Harry S. Truman

Harry S. Truman

Steven Otfinoski

AMERICA'S

33RD

PRESIDENT

Children's Press®
A Division of Scholastic Inc.
New York / Toronto / London / Auckland / Sydney
Mexico City / New Delhi / Hong Kong
Danbury, Connecticut

Library of Congress Cataloging-in-Publication Data

Otfinoski, Steven.
        Harry S. Truman / Steven Otfinoski.
            p. cm. — (Encyclopedia of presidents)
        Includes bibliographical references and index.
    ISBN 0-516-22974-5
    1. Truman, Harry S., 1884–1972—Juvenile literature. 2. Presidents—United
States—Biography—Juvenile literature. 3. United States—Politics and government—1945–1953—Juvenile literature. I. Title. II. Series.
E814.O84 2005
973.918'092—dc22   2004017771

Contents

Chapter 1

A Missouri Boyhood ——————————

Harry Truman did not seek to become president. When he was elected vice president in 1944, he believed that it would be the high point of his political career. Then fate thrust him into the presidency at a critical moment in American history. Truman found himself facing some of the gravest challenges any U.S. president has had to face. He confronted these challenges with courage, conviction, and wisdom. Indeed, in a survey of 58 presidential scholars in 2000, Truman was ranked fifth best of the 41 presidents rated.

Truman was born on May 8, 1884, in Lamar, in western Missouri. He was the oldest of three children of John Anderson Truman and Martha Ellen Young Truman, known as Mattie. They named their first child Harry after his mother's brother, his Uncle Harrison. His middle name was a problem. The Trumans wanted to use the name of one of the boy's grandfathers, but couldn't agree on which one. So they gave him the middle initial "S," which could stand for either Solomon Young or Anderson Shippe Truman. Truman is the only U.S. president with a middle initial that doesn't stand for a name.

On his mother's side, young Harry Truman's ancestors were of German descent, and on his father's side, they were English and Scots-Irish. Both sets of grandparents were farmers who came to Missouri from Kentucky in the 1840s. Harry's father, John Truman, was a livestock trader and part-time farmer. He was admired by his neighbors as a man of strong integrity who had a stubborn streak and a sometimes hot temper. John Truman was always looking for a way to rise above poverty and become financially secure, moving from one small Missouri town to another. Meanwhile, Harry's brother Vivian was born in 1886, and his sister Mary Jane was born three years later.

As a small boy, Harry Truman had trouble with his vision. When he was six, he was fitted for thick eyeglasses to correct his acute farsightedness. After that, he rarely played with the other boys, afraid he might break his glasses. Instead, he took piano lessons and read books. "To tell the truth, I was kind of a sissy," he confessed years later.

The same year Harry got his eyeglasses, the Truman family moved to Independence, Missouri. The town of 6,000 people was a pleasant but sleepy

A wedding portrait of Harry Truman's parents, Mattie and John Truman, taken in 1881.

Harry Truman at age 13.

place with the small-town characteristics of the Midwest and the South. Only 12 miles (19 kilometers) to the west, however, was Kansas City, the biggest and most important city in the region. In Independence, John Truman bought a house for his family with money he inherited from his father.

Soon after arriving in town, Truman first met a blue-eyed girl with blonde curls at the Presbyterian Sunday School. Her name was Elizabeth Wallace, known to all as Bess. Harry was six and Bess was five. Her family was one of the most prominent in Independence. She became the secret love of his life.

At school, Truman's teachers discovered that he was a diligent student. The older he got, the more he read. He later claimed that before he turned 14, he had read every book in the Independence public library. He especially enjoyed history and biography. His heroes were great military leaders, from Hannibal, who fought the Romans, to General Robert E. Lee, the hero of the South during the Civil War.

Bess Wallace was born in Independence on February 13, 1885, the first of four children and the only girl. Her father was a successful farmer and public official. Bess was something of a tomboy and excelled in several sports, including baseball and tennis. After high school, she went to study at Miss Barstow's Finishing School for Girls in Kansas City. Then in 1903, when Bess was 18, her father committed suicide. Bess returned home and took over the running of the Wallace household. She remained there until her marriage to Harry Truman 16 years later. After the wedding, the couple moved into the Wallace home where they lived the rest of their lives, except for their years in Washington, D.C.

Bess Wallace, the future wife of Harry Truman, at age 16.

☆ ☆ ☆

Working for a Living ———————————

Any hopes Harry Truman had of going to college were dashed in 1901, when he was 17. His father had made some unwise financial investments and lost most of his money. John Truman was forced to sell their house and move the family to a more modest home in Kansas City. Truman's only hope for going to college was to gain an appointment to the U.S. Military Academy at West Point, New York. Unfortunately, he failed the physical exam because of his poor eyesight.

So Harry Truman went to work to help support his family. He worked as a timekeeper with a railroad work gang and as a mailboy at a newspaper, the *Kansas City Star*. Then he spent two years as a bank clerk. His employers praised him for his hard work and initiative. For a time he roomed with another bank clerk, Arthur Eisenhower, whose younger brother Dwight would one day become a famous World War II general and be elected president.

While Harry was at work in Kansas City, his family had moved to Grandview, not far outside the city, where John Truman took charge of the 600-acre (240-hectare) farm that belonged to his mother-in-law. In 1906 the big farm became too much for John Truman to manage, and he summoned Harry to come and help him. Then 22 years old, Harry Truman was not interested in being a farmer, but he knew his family was counting on him. He left Kansas City and moved into the big farmhouse in Grandview. In the next ten years,

Truman learned how to farm, mastering the skills needed to grow crops and raise livestock. Years later he admitted that farm work gave him a strong work ethic and a habit of rising early that continued all his life.

By now he was seriously courting Bess Wallace, 10 miles (16 km) away in Independence, but visiting her was difficult. The Trumans did not own a car, and Harry had to take a roundabout route on trains and streetcars to reach Independence. In 1911 he proposed to Bess, but she gently turned him down. Undaunted, he continued to pursue her, sending her

Young bank clerk Harry Truman in his early 20s.

letters several times a week. Soon after she refused his proposal, he wrote, "I never was fool enough to think that a girl like you could ever care for a fellow like me, but I couldn't help telling you how I felt. . . . I have been so afraid that you were not even going to let me be your good friend. To be even in that class is something."

Truman rides a horse-drawn cultivator on the family farm in Grandview, Missouri, where he lived and worked for more than ten years.

In 1914 the year Harry Truman turned 30, John Truman suffered a hernia while trying to move a boulder. The hernia caused serious complications, and he died on November 2. Now Truman felt more chained to the farm than ever. Like his father, he began looking for investment opportunities to become financially independent. He invested in a zinc mine in Oklahoma and a promising oil-drilling scheme in Kansas City, but both ventures failed and left him deep in debt.

He found some relief from farm work in taking over his father's part-time position as road overseer in Jackson County. In 1915 he was also appointed postmaster of Grandview, another part-time position. Friendly and outgoing, Truman began attending Democratic political meetings in Kansas City. He admired and supported reform Democrat Woodrow Wilson, who was elected president in 1912 and again in 1916.

Off to War

While life in America was peaceful and prosperous, war had broken out in Europe in 1914, pitting the Central Powers (Germany, Austria-Hungary, and others) against an alliance that included Great Britain, France, and Russia. Soon known as the Great War (and later as World War I), the conflict cost millions of lives as armies used modern weapons to mow down enemy troops. By 1917

German submarines were sinking U.S. merchant ships along Europe's Atlantic coast. In April, President Wilson asked Congress for a declaration of war against Germany and the other Central Powers.

Truman, who had earlier served in the National Guard, was determined to do his part in the war. U.S. authorities were seeking recruits up to the age of 31 and also offered exemptions for farmers and men who provided their families' only support. At 33, farmer and family breadwinner Truman ignored the exemptions and enlisted with a newly formed National Guard artillery company, passing the physical exam in spite of his weak eyesight. His sister Mary Jane took over the operation of the farm in his absence.

Truman was elected second lieutenant by his fellow recruits. His unit was taken into the regular U.S. Army and trained at Fort Sill, Oklahoma. Truman quickly proved to be a good officer and an enterprising one. With Sergeant Eddie Jacobson, he operated the post canteen, which dispensed goods to the soldiers. Together they made it one of the most profitable canteens in the region.

After eight months of training, Truman's 129th Foot Artillery was sent to France, arriving in April 1918. Truman was promoted to captain, and for the first time in his life discovered his ability to lead others. His men called him "Captain Harry" and both respected and trusted him. He didn't let them down. He received demanding training in gunnery, which forced him to learn more mathematics than

Soldier Harry Truman on a postcard photograph he mailed to his family during his service.

he had ever studied in school. Then Truman and his men became part of a huge Allied offensive in the Meuse-Argonne valley. They dragged their heavy guns through miles of mud, ducked when German shells whistled overhead, and fired thousand of rounds at distant enemy positions. They performed well, and miraculously, only one man under Truman's command was killed. Then on November 11, 1918, the Germans signed an armistice agreement, and the guns on both sides fell silent.

Soon Truman's unit was withdrawn from the front. He visited Paris and France's Mediterranean shore, then returned home in the spring of 1919. His wartime experience became a turning point in his life. He decided once and for all that farming was a dead end for him. He sold off the livestock and equipment and rented the land to an outsider. He used his share of the proceeds to go into business in Kansas City. He and his army friend Eddie Jacobson leased a store in the city's bustling downtown area.

Even more important to Truman was Bess Wallace. Before he left for France she had agreed to marry him, and they agreed that the wedding would take place soon after he returned. They were married on June 28, 1919. Truman was 35 and Bess 34. With the war over, his farming days behind him, and his childhood sweetheart as his wife, Harry Truman felt ready to take hold of the American dream of success that had so far eluded him.

Harry and Bess Truman on their wedding day with members of the wedding party.

Chapter 2

A Failed Business ─────────────

In November 1919, Harry Truman and Eddie Jacobson opened their new store in Kansas City. Called Truman & Jacobson, it was a *haberdashery*, a men's clothing store that sold everything from underwear to neckties. The store did a booming business its first year, but late in 1920 farm prices fell drastically as a result of a nationwide economic depression. Kansas City's men no longer had spare money for fine shirts and neckties. By 1922 Truman & Jacobson could not pay its bills. It closed, leaving Truman and Jacobson $35,000 in debt. Truman refused to declare bankruptcy, preferring to repay every penny of his share of the debt. He succeeded, but it took him 15 years.

Truman & Jacobson had been a popular gathering place for their old army buddies. Among them was Jim Pendergast, whose

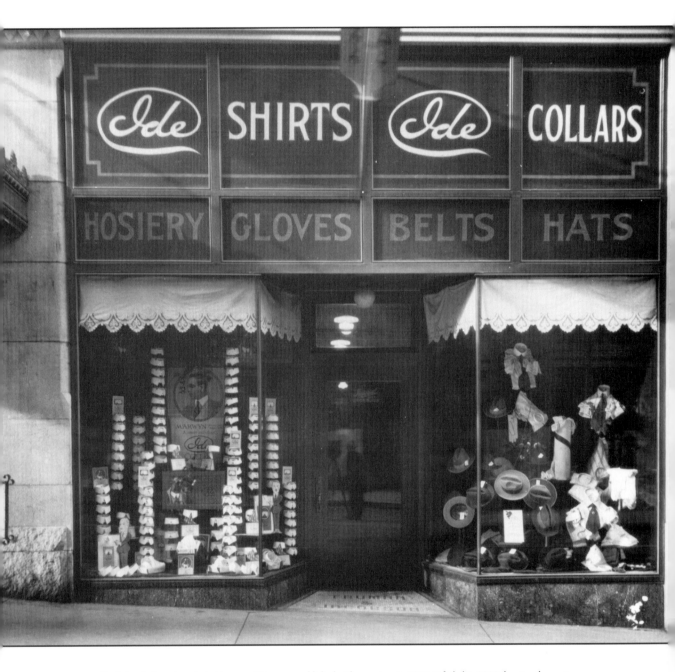

The haberdashery (men's clothing store) Truman established with a partner in 1919. It failed in 1922, leaving the partners deep in debt.

★ FROM SHOPKEEPER TO PRESIDENT ★

father, Mike, was active in Democratic politics. Jim's uncle, Tom Pendergast, was the powerful Democratic political boss of Kansas City. One day Jim brought his father into the store. Mike Pendergast was impressed by Truman, who was a war hero and an active Democrat with many friends in Independence and Grandview. The Pendergast machine was hoping to expand its power outside of Kansas City, and Mike Pendergast asked Truman to consider running in the 1922 election as one of three county judges in Jackson

Truman's political sponsor Tom Pendergast, the boss of the Kansas City Democratic machine.

County. When Truman & Jacobson closed, Truman needed a job badly, and he was attracted to politics. He agreed to run.

A Success in Politics

In his first campaign, Truman struggled with his lack of experience speaking in public. Still, with the support of the Pendergast organization, he won the judgeship for the eastern part of Jackson County. A county judge in Missouri was not a person

Thomas Joseph Pendergast

Tom Pendergast (1872–1945) was one of the most powerful of the Democratic political bosses who ran many American cities in the early 1900s. He was born in St. Joseph, Missouri, one of nine children of Irish immigrants. When he arrived in Kansas City in the 1890s, his older brother was already the Democratic boss of Kansas City. When the brother died, Tom took control of the machine.

Tom Pendergast did not seek public attention and never ran for office, preferring to work behind the scenes. He used his political power to help himself and his friends make huge profits from government contracts and collected protection money to allow illegal businesses to operate. During *Prohibition*, the years when the sale of alcohol was illegal, he allowed it to be sold in Kansas City in return for part of the profits. The machine also rigged elections to assure that its supporters would remain in power. Those elected were required to award big government contracts to companies that Pendergast controlled.

Despite his underhanded and illegal tactics, Pendergast did much good for the community. During the Great Depression in the 1930s, he provided jobs and income to thousands of citizens, and his organization left behind many handsome civic buildings. "We function," he once said, "as nearly as we can 100 percent by making people feel kindly toward us."

Pendergast was the model of virtue in his private life. He was faithful to his wife, attended Catholic mass every morning, and seldom drank. His only vice was gambling, and that proved to be his undoing. To cover his gambling debts, he collected one bribe too many and was caught. In 1939 he was convicted of tax evasion and served 12 months in prison. The power of his organization was broken, and he died quietly at home in 1945.

☆ ★ ☆

who heard court cases. The job was more like the position called "county commissioner" in other parts of the country. Its main responsibilities were to build and maintain county roads, bridges, and other public works. Truman did a thorough and efficient job and gained a reputation for honesty, even though his opponents pointed out that he was supported by Pendergast's big-city political machine.

Despite his popularity, Truman lost his bid for re-election in 1924. One reason was a disastrous involvement with the Ku Klux Klan. In February 1924, Truman joined the Klan to gain political support, without fully realizing that it was committed to preserving the power of white Protestants. Immediately, Klan leaders asked him to promise not to appoint any Jews or Catholics to political office. Horrified by the request, he resigned on the spot, making enemies of the Klan for opposing their policies. That fall, the Klan members worked hard to defeat Truman at the polls.

Also in 1924, the Trumans' daughter Mary Margaret was born. With a wife and daughter to support, Truman took any job he could find. He sold auto-club memberships for a time and was a partner in a small bank. Like the men's shop, it failed.

In 1926 Truman ran for presiding judge of the county and won. Four years later he was re-elected. For eight years he skillfully supervised many public works and appointed hundreds to county jobs. Despite his connection to

Bess Truman and the Trumans' baby daughter Margaret in 1924.

Pendergast, not a breath of scandal or corruption sullied his career. Even Tom Pendergast had to acknowledge Truman's integrity. When Truman refused to appoint Pendergast's favored contractors, the old boss said, "He's the contrariest cuss in Missouri." By the time Truman left the judgeship, Jackson County had more than 200 miles (320 km) of new concrete roads, allowing farmers to carry their crops and livestock to market in any weather. In addition, new county courthouses were under construction in Kansas City and Independence.

Truman was hoping that Pendergast would help him gain higher office, but was disappointed when the boss passed him over and nominated others to run for governor and for Congress. Truman remained patient, however, and in 1934, Pendergast offered Truman the best opportunity of all—a chance to run for the U.S. Senate.

This time Pendergast needed Truman as much as Truman needed him. By 1934 reformers in the Democratic party were going after the boss of Kansas City. Pendergast needed a candidate who was not suspected of corruption and who could win election. The Democratic nominee was chosen in a tough primary election among Democratic hopefuls. Although well known in western Missouri, Truman had to introduce himself to the rest of the state. With Pendergast's help, he managed to win the primary, and in November he defeated the Republican candidate by more than 260,000 votes.

Senator Truman

When Truman arrived in Washington, he had to overcome the reputation of being "the senator from Pendergast." He soon won over other senators by his forthright manner and his talent for making friends. Senator Truman was a staunch supporter of President Franklin Roosevelt's New Deal, the ambitious effort then under way to address the Great Depression. The president hoped to turn the U.S. economy around and to provide jobs and assistance to millions who were jobless, homeless, or hungry.

Truman was appointed to the Interstate Commerce Committee. One of the committee's responsibilities was to oversee the charges railroads made to haul freight and passengers. Truman led an investigation that uncovered illegal activities—and implicated some of his old political friends in Missouri. Truman refused to look the other way. He urged prosecution of the accused to the full extent of the law.

In 1939 Tom Pendergast was convicted for tax evasion and sentenced to prison. With his the conviction, the Pendergast organization began to fall apart. For Truman, the machine's downfall came at the worst possible time. He was up for re-election to the Senate in 1940 and faced stiff competition from reformers in his own party. Without the support of the Pendergast organization, he lacked

Harry, 16-year-old Margaret, and Bess Truman during his uphill campaign for re-election to the Senate in 1940. A portrait of President Franklin D. Roosevelt is in the background.

funds and workers to mount an effective campaign. Truman called on his many Missouri friends for support. With Bess and Margaret (then 16 years old), he barnstormed the state, selling himself as never before. Through sheer grit and determination, he managed to win the nomination and then the general election.

World War II had erupted in Europe in September 1939. German armies invaded Poland and soon overran a large part of Europe. In Asia, Japan was also on the march. At first, Americans hoped to stay out of the conflict, but President Roosevelt knew that the country had to prepare to support Britain, France, the Soviet Union, and other Allied nations. He greatly increased spending for defense. After a tour of military sites and plants, Harry Truman reported signs of widespread corruption and waste. Government military contracts were being awarded to large companies with political influence, and they were abusing the government's trust. Based on his findings, the Senate set up the Special Committee to Investigate the National Defense Program in March 1941. As head of the committee, Truman continued his investigations and helped reform the system. His efforts saved the government untold millions of dollars and brought the senator from Missouri into the national spotlight.

The 1944 Presidential Election —————

The United States entered the war in December 1941, after Japanese bombers attacked the U.S. naval base at Pearl Harbor, in Hawaii. By 1944 millions of Americans were fighting Japan in the Pacific and Germany in Europe. At home, millions more worked in defense industries. As the presidential election approached, Democrats agreed to nominate President Franklin Roosevelt to a fourth term, believing that Americans wanted his leadership during the wartime crisis.

The party disagreed about Roosevelt's vice-presidential candidate, however. Henry A. Wallace, the current vice president, was a strong supporter of Roosevelt's New Deal policies, which had greatly increased the size and power of the federal government. Yet many Democrats believed that his strong support for big government would turn voters away from the Democratic ticket. They wanted a vice president who would not divide the country and give ammunition to the Republicans.

Two leading contenders for the job were Supreme Court Justice William O. Douglas, a liberal like Wallace, and former senator James F. Byrnes of South Carolina, a conservative. Roosevelt considered both men friends and was reluctant to choose between them. Finally, Robert Hannegan, chairman of the Democratic

National Committee, proposed Harry Truman as a compromise candidate. Truman was a moderate who could appeal to both conservatives and liberals.

When the Democratic convention convened in July, Truman came prepared to give a nominating speech for his friend James Byrnes, believing that Byrnes had the nomination sewed up. When Truman learned that he himself was the choice of Democratic leaders, he said he didn't want the nomination. He was happy in the Senate and didn't want to become vice president. When he learned

The Vice Presidency

It is not surprising that Harry Truman did not want to be vice president. He knew the vice president has little influence compared to that of a senator. According to the Constitution, the main responsibility of the vice president is to preside over meetings of the Senate. Even there, Senate custom would not let the vice president speak on the issues, and he could cast a vote only if the Senate was tied. Any other responsibilities depended on the will of the president, and most presidents had not made much use of their backups.

Since Truman's presidency, many vice presidents have received responsibility and have participated in major executive decisions. Still, the vice president's most important duty is to stand ready to serve as president if the current president dies, resigns, or is removed from office. Fourteen vice presidents have become presidents, eight of them after the death of a president.

☆ ☆ ☆

After being chosen as Roosevelt's vice-presidential running mate in 1944, Truman has lunch with the president at the Roosevelt estate in Hyde Park, New York.

that the president himself wanted him to run, however, Truman realized he couldn't refuse and agreed to accept the nomination.

Truman won the nomination on the second ballot. In November, Roosevelt and Truman were elected handily over the Republicans Thomas E. Dewey of New York and John W. Bricker of Ohio.

A Brief Vice Presidency

Roosevelt and Truman were inaugurated on January 20, 1945. From the beginning, Truman found it difficult to adjust to the vice presidency. He quickly learned that he was not consulted or informed about important decisions of the Roosevelt administration. In the first months, he met with President Roosevelt only twice. Although he enjoyed presiding over his old colleagues in the Senate, he could no longer be a force in making legislative policy there. "I am trying to make a job out of the vice presidency," he wrote, "and it's quite a chore."

Then, twelve weeks after the inauguration, on April 12, Truman was visiting Speaker of the House Sam Rayburn after adjourning the Senate. At about 5 p.m., he received an urgent telephone message to come to the White House. When he arrived, he was taken to the study of first lady Eleanor Roosevelt. "Harry," she said, "the president is dead." Roosevelt had suffered a fatal *stroke* (stoppage of blood supply to the brain) at his presidential retreat in Warm Springs, Georgia.

"Is there anything I can do for you?" Truman asked the first lady.

"Is there anything *we* can do for *you*?" she answered. "For you are the one in trouble now."

Truman is sworn in as president at the White House on April 12, 1945, hours after President Roosevelt's death. Bess and Margaret Truman are at the right.

At 7:09 p.m., with Bess and Margaret at his side, Harry Truman was sworn in as president by Chief Justice Harlan Stone in a private White House ceremony. Now he was the 33rd president of the United States.

Chapter 3

An Accidental President

The day after he was sworn in as president, Truman met with reporters covering the White House. "I don't know whether you fellows ever had a load of hay fall on you," Truman told them, "but when they told me yesterday what had happened, I felt like the moon, the stars, and all the planets had fallen on me."

Truman had reason to feel overwhelmed. No vice president sworn in after his predecessor's death has faced more daunting challenges. Overseas, millions of Americans were still engaged in battle. In Europe, Nazi Germany was on the verge of collapse, but much of Europe lay in ruins. Worse, the armies of the Soviet Union, a powerful ally of the United States during the war, seemed determined to make the countries of Eastern Europe part of its own great empire. In the Pacific, the Allies were closing in on Japan, but that country's leaders seemed unlikely to surrender, training children and old men to fight if the Allies invaded their homeland.

Truman also had reason to question his own ability to manage the situation. Since he was not part of President Roosevelt's inner circle, he did not know those most involved in making vital decisions about conducting the war and planning for peace. He had never met the famous leaders of America's main allies, Prime Minister Winston Churchill of Great Britain and Premier Joseph Stalin of the Soviet Union. Now Truman would have to make fateful decisions about the war effort and deal with Allied leaders himself. Many American political and military leaders doubted that Truman could handle the job. To them he seemed a mediocre man at a time that demanded special brilliance. "It was a terrible thing to have to take on," he wrote about the presidency, "[but] maybe that made me work harder."

The first decision he faced concerned the San Francisco Conference on the United Nations (UN), scheduled to begin in only twelve days. Roosevelt and Churchill had worked hard to establish the international organization, hoping that it could help avoid future conflicts. Now that Roosevelt was dead, should the conference to write a United Nations Charter be postponed? Truman decided that it should go on as scheduled. The charter prepared by the conference was signed by participating nations on June 26, 1945, and Truman appeared personally to express his support for the new organization.

After Russian and American armies met in Germany in April 1945, the troops celebrate their victories. Ten days later, Germany formally surrendered, ending the war in Europe.

As Soviet forces closed in on Berlin, the German capital, German dictator Adolf Hitler committed suicide on April 30. A week later, Germany surrendered, ending the war in Europe. In the Pacific, the war continued. The Allies' calls for Japan to surrender went unanswered. Allied troops were planning an invasion of Japan itself, but U.S. general George Marshall predicted that more than 250,000 American troops would be killed before Japan could be overcome. At this point, Truman learned about the Manhattan Project, which was racing to prepare a new "superweapon," the atomic bomb. Its supporters hoped it would be ready in case it could be used to shorten the war against Japan.

The Potsdam Conference

In mid-July, Truman left Washington to face the first major test of his presidency—a meeting with British prime minister Churchill and Soviet premier Stalin. It began July 17 in Potsdam, Germany, just outside Berlin. The leaders had two major issues to discuss: planning to carry on the war against Japan, and planning the future of Eastern Europe and occupied Germany.

Truman arrived at Potsdam nervous and apprehensive, but he soon relaxed. He took a liking to Stalin, who reminded him of his old mentor Tom Pendergast. He was less taken with Churchill. "Churchill talks all the time and Stalin just grunts but you know what he means," he wrote in a letter to his mother and sister. During the conference, on July 21, 1945, Truman received word that the first atomic bomb had been set off successfully in the desert near Alamogordo, New Mexico. He later admitted that "I did not like the weapon," but he understood that it might be used to end the war quickly and save lives.

On July 24, he sent an order to the U.S. command to prepare for the possible use of the atomic bomb on Japan, and he informed Churchill of his decision. Later that afternoon Truman casually told Stalin that the United States had "a new

Harry Truman shakes hands with British prime minister Winston Churchill (left) and Soviet premier Joseph Stalin (right) at the Potsdam Conference in July 1945.

weapon of unusual destructive force." Stalin seemed not to understand the importance of the remark, but in fact he knew quite a bit about the secret U.S. bomb project. Soviet spies in the United States had been sending information about it to their government. Soviet scientists were at work on their own atomic bomb.

Truman got Stalin's commitment for Soviet help in the war against Japan. The leaders also agreed that parts of Germany's prewar territory should be given to Poland and the Soviet Union. They agreed on the division of Germany into four occupation sectors, to be managed by the United States, Britain, France, and the Soviet Union. The city of Berlin, in the Soviet sector, would also be divided and occupied by all four nations. This agreement would soon lead to further disputes.

War's End

At 8:15 a.m. on August 6, 1945, a U.S. B-29 bomber, the *Enola Gay*, dropped the first atomic bomb ever used for war on the Japanese city of Hiroshima. Some 75,000 people, mostly civilians, were killed instantly. When no word of surrender came from the Japanese government, a second bomb was dropped on the seaport of Nagasaki three days later. Another 40,000 people were killed. (Thousands more would die in the coming months from burns and radiation sickness.) Reeling from the two attacks, the Japanese opened peace negotiations. On August 14, Japanese emperor Hirohito surrendered unconditionally to U.S.

Inset, a huge mushroom cloud rises over Nagasaki, Japan, on August 9, 1945, as an atomic bomb explodes. Above, the remains of the city days afterward. More than 40,000 people were killed.

representatives. The formal surrender ceremony was held September 2, marking the end of World War II.

Truman's decision to drop atomic bombs on Japanese cities became his most controversial act as president. His critics claimed that he had unleashed a new power on Earth that might one day destroy all humanity. Some believed that the Japanese were closer to surrendering than U.S. leaders knew. Truman's supporters pointed out that Japan was controlled by military fanatics who hoped to see their people fight to the last man. They suggested that an Allied invasion of Japan might have resulted in the deaths of five or ten times the number killed by the bombs.

In some respects, Truman's decision was deeply personal. He had seen combat and knew that hundreds of soldiers and sailors were dying every day. He

Hiroshima and Nagasaki

Decades after they were attacked, the Japanese cities of Hiroshima and Nagasaki remain the only two cities in the world to experience the devastating power of the atomic bomb. They have been rebuilt, but both have set aside parks to commemorate the death and destruction of August 1945. Thousands of visitors visit the Hiroshima Peace Memorial Museum each year. In addition, a conference center provides a setting for international discussions about war and peace, and about the control of nuclear weapons.

☆ ★ ☆

Joyful crowds gather outside the White House to celebrate the end of World War II after the Japanese announce their surrender on August 14, 1945.

knew that if he refused to use the terrible new weapon, he would have to answer to the American people for lengthening the war and increasing casualties. He never expressed any doubt that he had made the right and necessary decision.

Domestic Matters

With the war over, Truman turned his attention to domestic matters. His first concern was the millions of U.S. servicemen and women who were returning home. The Servicemen's Readjustment Act, more popularly known as the G.I. Bill of Rights, had been passed by Congress in 1944. Its purpose was to help returning servicemen and women make the difficult transition to civilian life more smoothly. It provided veterans with funds for a college education or vocational training, low-interest loans to purchase new homes and businesses, and unemployment benefits. Truman made sure that the program was funded and working smoothly.

He also worked with his economic advisers to help retool American business and industry for peace. During the war, factories had been devoted to making planes, tanks, arms, and other military necessities. Now, thousands of consumer items, including automobiles, were in short supply. The demand of consumers for these scarce products caused prices to rise, so government economists worked to reduce *inflation*. Truman also worked to expand Social Security, the New Deal program that withheld taxes from workers in order to pay benefits to those who retired or were disabled. He also continued Roosevelt's public works programs to build hydroelectric plants to produce cheap electricity from the power of major rivers.

Truman broke entirely new ground in social reform. Although he had grown up in an atmosphere of racial prejudice, he knew it was wrong, and he believed that as president it was his duty to create a more just American society. The Fair Employment Practices Committee (FEPC) had been created by Roosevelt in 1943. It outlawed racial discrimination in the hiring of workers in defense industries. In 1946, Congress refused to appropriate money to continue the FEPC, and it closed. Truman began a campaign to revive it and make it a permanent agency. In 1947 he became the first president to address the National Association for the Advancement of Colored People (the NAACP). He told them, "Many of our people still suffer the indignity of insult, the harrowing fear of intimidation, and, I regret to say, of physical and mob violence. . . . We cannot wait another decade or generation to remedy these evils. We must work as never before to cure them now."

As hard as the Truman administration worked, many Americans were unhappy with the results. In the 1946 congressional elections, Republicans gained control of Congress for the first time in 16 years. When Congress met in 1947, conservative Republicans and Democrats blocked Truman's domestic programs, including the revival of the FEPC, and tried to push through more conservative legislation of their own.

President Truman and his daughter Margaret vote in the 1946 elections. At age 22, Margaret was voting for the first time.

Labor Strikes

During the war, wages and prices were controlled by the government. Soon after the war, workers began clamoring for better pay. They were led by the major industrial unions. In April 1946, coal miners went on strike. The following month, railroad workers threatened to strike as well. Truman threatened to take action against the railroad workers. If they went on strike, he said, he would put the railroads under federal government control. The strike was postponed for five days, but then the workers defied the president and walked out. All rail transportation stopped and the nation was paralyzed. Truman went before Congress and asked for authorization to draft the striking workers into the armed forces. Minutes later, the strike ended and workers went back to their jobs. The coal strike was also soon settled. Truman had won the battle against striking unions, but at a high cost. The unions, long powerful supporters of the Democratic party, withdrew their support of the president.

The next year, the new Congress expressed widespread dissatisfaction with aggressive labor unions. It passed the Taft-Hartley Act, amending earlier legislation protecting unions and their members. This act strengthened the rights of employers in negotiating union contracts and outlawed union abuses. President Truman vetoed the act, but Congress overrode his veto, passing it by two-thirds majorities in both houses.

In this hostile environment, Truman felt increasingly isolated. When Bess and Margaret made lengthy visits to Independence, he was left alone in the White House. He missed them terribly and referred to the president's mansion in one letter to Bess as "the great white sepulcher of ambitions and reputations." To another colleague he gave this terse advice, "If you want a friend in Washington, get a dog."

Chapter 4

The Truman Doctrine and the Marshall Plan

At war's end, the United States faced challenges overseas. It soon became clear that the Soviet Union was installing puppet governments loyal to Soviet Communism in Eastern Europe. Between 1945 and 1948, Poland, Czechoslovakia, Hungary, and Yugoslavia all became Communist states. Truman feared that the Soviets would turn their sights to Southern and Western Europe. He was particularly concerned about Greece and Turkey, where Communist insurgents threatened to overthrow the existing governments. In a speech to Congress in March 1947, Truman asked it to supply aid to Greece and Turkey. He went on to declare that the United States would come to the aid of any country threatened by Communist domination. This statement became known as the Truman Doctrine. It helped begin the Cold War, the war of words and policy between the United States and the Soviet Union that would continue for the next 40 years.

In 1947 Truman appointed General George C. Marshall as secretary of state. Marshall, who had served as army chief of staff through World War II, was widely admired for his wisdom and skill. Now Marshall pointed out that the countries of Western Europe, which had suffered heavy damage during the war, were in economic and political danger. Unless they had the resources to rebuild their war-torn towns and industries, they too might fall under Soviet domination. In June 1947, three months after the announcement of the Truman Doctrine, Marshall proposed a huge economic aid program for Europe, providing assistance not just to Allied nations, but also to former enemies Germany and Italy and to Communist nations in Eastern Europe.

In April 1948, Congress budgeted $5.3 billion for the Marshall Plan. Sixteen nations received aid, including Italy and West Germany (the portion of Germany formerly occupied by the United States, Britain, and France). The Soviet Union and its allies in Eastern Europe refused to participate. By 1952 the plan had distributed $13.5 billion. It succeeded in reviving Western Europe's economy and reducing the threat of European Communism.

George Catlett Marshall

George Marshall (1880–1959) played a central role in planning Allied strategy during World War II. Then, as the first professional soldier ever to serve as secretary of state, he played a major part in Europe's economic recovery after the war.

Marshall was born in Uniontown, Pennsylvania, and settled on a military career as a young man. After graduating from the Virginia Military Institute in 1902, he joined the U.S. Army. During World War I Marshall became chief of operations for the U.S. First Army. He later was a leading planner of U.S. offensives in France, including the Meuse-Argonne offensive, in which Captain Harry Truman played a small role.

On September 1, 1939, the day German armies invaded Poland, Marshall became Army Chief of Staff. After the United States entered the war in 1941, Marshall was eager to take command the army in Europe, but President Roosevelt believed he was too valuable in Washington, and kept him there through the war. In 1944, *Time* magazine named Marshall "Man of the Year" for his role in arming the nation and helping plan Allied strategy.

In 1947 President Truman appointed him secretary of state. After setting up the Marshall Plan, Marshall helped establish the North Atlantic Treaty Organization (NATO), the mutual defense alliance between the United States and countries in Western Europe. Marshall resigned as secretary of state in 1949, but he returned to the Truman cabinet in 1951, serving briefly as secretary of defense. In 1953 he was awarded the Nobel Peace Prize for his work on the Marshall Plan.

☆ ☆ ☆

The Marshall Plan helped reconstruct much of Western Europe, including Germany. In West Berlin, the badly damaged German capital, a worker clears the rubble of bombed-out buildings. The sign says "Berlin emergency program with the assistance of the Marshall Plan."

The Berlin Airlift ————————————————

Germany became a major cause of conflict between the Western powers and the Soviet Union. In the Western sector, Britain, France, and the United States hoped to end Allied occupation and create an independent German government. The Soviets refused to cooperate or to make their Eastern sector part of the new nation. In 1948, as the differences between east and west grew larger, conflict broke out over West Berlin.

Berlin was surrounded by Soviet-occupied Germany, about 110 miles (175 km) from the Western zone, but it was governed by the four major powers. On June 24, 1948, the Soviets announced a *blockade* on West Berlin, blocking the train lines and highways that brought food, fuel, and other supplies from western Germany to the American, British, and French sectors of Berlin. Without these supplies, the residents would soon starve or freeze unless they accepted the rule of Soviet-controlled Germany.

Truman was faced with a serious crisis. How could the Western powers supply the isolated city without beginning a war with the Soviets? He ordered that U.S. military forces organize a huge airlift to carry supplies to the belea-guered city until the Soviets gave up their blockade. Soon U.S. transport planes were landing at the airport in western Berlin every few minutes, bringing food, fuel, clothing, medicines, and other needed supplies. The Soviets threatened military action against the planes, but never actually interfered. After eleven long months, the Soviets ended their blockade on May 12, 1949, allowing supplies to reach Berlin over land. Because of the shortages, however, the airlift continued until September 30. In more than 16 months, the Western allies delivered nearly 300,000 planeloads of supplies—about 2.3 million tons (2.1 million metric tons). Truman had faced down a serious threat and demonstrated that the West would not abandon Berlin.

The aftermath of World War II brought strife to another part of the world as well. Near the end of the war, Allied forces discovered German death camps where authorities had executed millions of people they considered undesirable. They made a special effort to exterminate Jews, systematically killing millions from Germany and from countries overrun by German troops. After the war, Jews sought a homeland in the Middle East. In November 1947, the United Nations voted to partition the land of Palestine into Arab and Jewish areas. Jews from Europe and other parts of the world flocked to the new territory, and in May 1948, the new Jewish state of Israel was established. Truman quickly recognized the new state despite the objections of displaced Palestinians and surrounding Arab states. The United States would remain a firm ally of Israel for more than half a century.

Planes landing in Berlin with supplies sometimes dropped candy bars in handkerchief parachutes to waiting children in a city park.

Political Storm Clouds

By 1948 millions in the United States had lost their enthusiasm for Harry Truman. Despite his accomplishments in foreign affairs, he had made little headway on important issues at home. Decent housing was still scarce and expensive. Prices for everyday necessities were rising much more rapidly than wages. Truman had little influence with the Republican-controlled Congress, and he had angered people on both sides of the issues. For example, union members blamed him for taking tough actions to end strikes, while businessmen remembered his veto of the anti-union Taft-Hartley Act.

The president had angered others by his firm stand on civil rights. In 1948, he ordered the desegregation of the U.S. armed forces, ending the practice of forming all-black and all-white military units. In addition, he proposed a ten-point program for protecting the civil rights of African Americans. Conservative Southern Democrats condemned both his actions and his proposals.

Truman announced that he would run for a full term as president in 1948, but many Democrats believed he couldn't be elected. Top party leaders advised him not to run. Others hoped that World War II general Dwight Eisenhower would run for president on the Democratic ticket, but Eisenhower refused. As the Democratic convention approached, Truman's chances of victory seemed very slim.

"Give 'Em Hell, Harry!"

When the Democratic National Convention met in Philadelphia in July 1948, the party had been in power for nearly 16 years, most of them under the leadership of President Franklin D. Roosevelt. Now, in their first convention since Roosevelt's death, Democrats were divided and quarrelsome. Liberals urged the party to support programs to extend Roosevelt's New Deal, increasing government aid to the poor and protection of civil rights for African Americans. Southern conservatives demanded that the party cut back its programs and leave enforcement of civil rights to state governments.

Southern delegates, angered by a strong civil rights plank proposed for the party *platform* (a statement of its principles and goals), walked out of the convention. They formed the States' Rights party (nicknamed the "Dixiecrats") and nominated South Carolina senator Strom Thurmond as their presidential candidate. Later, a group of liberal Democrats formed the Progressive party and nominated former vice president Henry A. Wallace for president. It seemed that the ruling party was falling apart.

Truman stood between the party extremes. He urged Democrats to patch up their differences and unite behind his candidacy. Although many delegates were not enthusiastic, they nominated him for president on the first ballot. They nominated Senator Alben Barkley of Kentucky for vice president.

In sharp contrast to the Democrats, the Republicans united solidly behind their presidential candidate, New York governor Thomas E. Dewey. Dewey had run for president against Roosevelt in 1944 and lost, but Republicans believed he could beat the vulnerable Truman.

Truman was down, but he was far from out. Soon after the Democratic convention, he went on the attack. On July 26, 1948, he called a special session of Congress and presented them with a program of Democratic initiatives, including a price-control program to reduce inflation, a tax on corporations' excess profits, and an increase in the minimum wage. Predictably, the Republican-controlled Congress refused to pass any of his proposals. This gave Truman the chance to campaign not against Tom Dewey, but against what he called the "do-nothing Republican Congress."

With little support from the press or the public opinion polls, Truman took his case directly to the people. On September 17, he began an old-fashioned "whistle-stop tour," crisscrossing the country by train, and speaking at every stop. With Bess and Margaret by his side, he traveled 32,000 miles (51,500 km) and delivered more than 250 speeches by October 31. People crowded around his railroad car to hear Truman rip into the Republicans. They admired his fighting spirit and friendly manner. "Give 'em hell, Harry!" became a popular cry from the crowd.

As the 1948 election approached, all signs pointed to a defeat for President Truman. In this cartoon, Republican candidate Tom Dewey is confident and Truman looks concerned.

Newspaper columnists doubted Truman's old-fashioned campaign would work. Dewey seemed much more "presidential," and it seemed voters were ready for a change. Even Madge Wallace, Truman's tart-tongued mother-in-law, called Dewey "that nice man" and told the press, "I know dozens of men better qualified to be in Mr. Truman's place in the White House."

As election day approached, nearly all the opinion polls predicted a Dewey victory, and Republicans were full of confidence. Even when early election returns showed Truman ahead, they still expected a Dewey landslide. As election night wore on, however, Truman's lead grew wider. By morning, the result was clear. Truman, the underdog, received 24 million votes to Dewey's 22 million. Splinter party candidates Thurmond and Wallace each won about 1.2 million votes. In the electoral college, Truman had a clear majority, with 303 votes to Dewey's 189 and Thurmond's 39.

The morning after the election, Truman was on his way from Independence to Washington by train. During a stop in St. Louis, his train was surrounded by celebrating supporters. He appeared at the back of the train with an early edition of the *Chicago Tribune*, a leading Republican newspaper. The banner headline, printed before full election results were in, proclaimed, "DEWEY DEFEATS TRUMAN." Truman showed the mistaken headline to the crowd with a huge grin on his face.

The day after the 1948 election, a jubilant Harry Truman holds up an early edition of the *Chicago Tribune*, which mistakenly proclaims his defeat.

NATO

Truman had proved that he could win the presidency on his own, and he was quick to exercise his presidential mandate. In his inaugural address he focused on four main points, all concerning foreign policy. First, he pledged that the United States would continue to support the United Nations. Second, he promised the Marshall Plan would go on helping to rebuild Europe.

In his third point, Truman announced a new development. He and Secretary of State Marshall had been working with U.S. allies to form the North Atlantic Treaty Organization (NATO). Truman explained the need for an alliance with longtime allies in Europe to guard against Soviet aggression there. The treaty was signed on April 4, 1949, by twelve nations, including Canada, Great Britain, France, and the United States. It was the first defensive alliance the United States had made since 1778. General Dwight D. Eisenhower, who had commanded Allied forces in Europe during World War II, was named NATO's first supreme commander. Before the year ended, the need for the alliance was demonstrated when the Soviet Union became the second nation to detonate an atomic bomb.

Truman's fourth point was the announcement of a new international program to "make the benefits of our scientific advances and industrial progress available for the improvement and growth of underdeveloped areas." This so-called Point Four Program was approved by Congress in 1950 and provided technical and scientific assistance to developing nations for many years.

The inaugural address was hailed by the press as the best speech of Truman's career, proving again that his foreign policy had wide support. Yet Truman's domestic program continued to stall. He proposed an agenda of programs called the Fair Deal, including increased aid to education, a federal health

TRUMAN IS INAUGURATED

Truman and his popular vice president, Alben Barkley, on inauguration day in January 1949.

insurance plan, and greater expenditures for public housing to ease a severe housing shortage. Although Democrats won a majority in both houses of Congress in the 1948 elections, Republicans and Southern Democrats in Congress combined to defeat most of Truman's proposals.

Life in the White House

For all the challenges he faced, Truman still found time for relaxation. He spent much of his leisure time with his wife and daughter. They enjoyed each other's company so much that White House employees often referred to them as "the Three Musketeers."

Truman was not much of an athlete. His favorite sport was horseshoes, and he had horseshoe pits dug into the White House lawn. His favorite vacation spot

First Lady Bess Truman

Bess Truman's most outstanding characteristic as first lady was her refusal to be anything other than what she was, a warm but very private woman. She was a striking contrast to first lady Eleanor Roosevelt, who had traveled the globe and often spoke out on political issues. Bess rarely spoke in public, and her travels were confined to visits with her family in Independence. Yet she was a self-possessed—and opinionated—woman.

Harry Truman called his wife "the Boss," and she ran the Truman household while Truman ran the country. In addition, she was a true partner to her husband in his political career. She accompanied him on long campaign trips and had worked on his office staff when he was in the Senate. When he became president, she served on many national charity committees and helped to renovate the White House, which was in sad disrepair.

Their long and loving marriage ended with his death in 1972. She died ten years later on October 18, 1982, at the age of 97.

☆ ★ ☆

was Key West, Florida, where he enjoyed swimming, lying on the beach, and playing poker with old friends. During his breaks, he worked at the Key West Naval Station, which was dubbed the "Little White House." In Florida, Truman wore bright Hawaiian print shirts, which became known as "Truman shirts."

In the White House, Truman enjoyed playing the piano, a hobby he had pursued since he took piano lessons as a boy. He played classical pieces and popular songs. At public gatherings, supporters often urged him to play "The Missouri Waltz." It was not one of the president's favorites, but it remained a crowd pleaser. Truman had collected many recordings of classical music and enjoyed listening to them. He also continued to read histories and biographies.

Truman was usually mild and friendly, but occasionally he lost control of his temper. In December 1950, Margaret Truman, who had studied as a singer for years, gave her first recital in Washington. The review that appeared the next morning

Margaret Truman on the night of her recital at Constitution Hall. President Truman, angered by a bad review of her performance, sent a stinging letter to the music critic.

in the *Washington Post* was highly critical of Margaret's performance. Truman was furious. He dashed off a letter to the reviewer, Paul Hume. Near the end, he said, "Some day I hope to meet you. When that happens you'll need a new nose [and] a lot of beefsteak for black eyes!"

Chapter 5

"Truman's War"

During 1950 the battle between the Communist world and the free world shifted to Asia. On June 25, the troops of Communist North Korea invaded South Korea, an ally of the United States. Truman was at home in Independence when he learned of the attack.

Korea had been ruled by Japan since 1895. At the end of World War II, Allied forces occupied the Korean peninsula south of the 38th parallel, and Soviet troops occupied the territory north of that line. The United Nations tried to organize elections to establish a single government for a unified nation, but North and South Korean representatives could not agree on ground rules. In 1948 South Korea held elections and established the Republic of Korea, with support and advice from the United States. Soon afterward, North Koreans established the Democratic Republic of Korea. Both nations began military buildups.

After most U.S. and Soviet troops withdrew, the two Korean governments began to drift toward war. Finally, in June 1950, North Korea attacked.

Truman and his advisers viewed the invasion as an instance of Soviet aggression. They were determined to resist the takeover of South Korea. The U.S. government convinced the United Nations to pass a resolution ordering North

British newspapers report on U.S. actions after North Korea's invasion of South Korea in June 1950. The three-year war there caused the deaths of more than 50,000 U.S. troops.

Korean forces to leave the South. When they ignored the resolution, the United Nations authorized a coalition of member nations to help South Korea defend its territory. The force, made up largely of U.S. units, was commanded by U.S. general Douglas Mac-Arthur, one of the heroes of fighting in the Pacific during World War II.

Within four months, the UN forces regained all South Korean territory and occupied much of North Korea. At this point, the Communist government of the People's Republic of China sent troops to support North Korea. It appeared that the conflict might become another world war.

The reinforced armies in the North drove UN forces south once again and captured Seoul, the South Korean capital. MacArthur counterattacked, and regained Seoul. At this point, the war settled into a deadly stalemate, with the line of battle wavering near the 38th parallel, the border before the war.

Fast Facts

THE KOREAN WAR

Who: Communist North Korea and its Chinese allies against the Republic of South Korea and UN forces led by the United States

When: June 25, 1950, to July 27, 1953

Why: North Korea attacked South Korea, seeking to unify the country under Communist rule. The United States and other UN members sent troops to help South Korean forces defend their territory.

Where: North and South Korea

Outcome: An armistice agreement was signed July 27, 1953, defining the border between North and South Korea near the 38th parallel. No permanent peace treaty was ever signed, and relations between the two Koreas remained tense and dangerous for more than 50 years.

The United States never officially declared war on North Korea. The conflict was considered a "police action" under UN control, even though the military command and about 90 percent of all troops were American. As American casualties increased, the public became weary of the war, and Congress became reluctant to support it. The press began referring to it as "Truman's War."

The Anti-Communist Movement ─────────

Even before World War II ended, Americans began to fear the power and aggressive intentions of international Communism, led by the Soviet Union. When the Soviets began creating puppet states in Eastern Europe after the war, fears increased. Then in 1949, Communist leader Mao Zedong took power in China after a civil war against the Nationalist government, which was an ally of the United States. It seemed that Communism was on the march in Europe and in Asia.

In the United States, anti-Communism became a powerful political force. Republicans raised questions about U.S. cooperation with the Soviet Union during World War II, suggesting that Democratic leaders might be "soft on Communism." They asked why the Truman administration had not done more to prevent the Communist takeover of Poland, Czechoslovakia, Hungary, and most of all, China.

Anti-Communists also raised questions about the loyalty of individual Americans. In the House Un-American Activities Committee, Congressman

Richard Nixon investigated former diplomat Alger Hiss and produced evidence that he was once a member of a Soviet spy ring. Then in 1950, the FBI arrested Julius Rosenberg and his wife and charged them with sending top-secret information about U.S. research on nuclear weapons to the Soviet Union. Fear about spies and Communist subversion at home rose to a fever pitch.

In 1950, Congress proposed the Internal Security Act, which called for the identification and prosecution of American Communists and also allowed for the detention of anyone suspected of sabotage or espionage. Truman vetoed the bill, claiming that it infringed on personal liberties, but Congress overrode his veto and the bill became law.

The most vocal anti-Communist of all was Wisconsin Republican senator Joseph McCarthy. McCarthy claimed to have lists of high-ranking government employees (most of them Democrats) who were or once had been Communists. In public hearings he grilled and humiliated those who would not cooperate with his committee.

Truman had demonstrated his opposition to Communism in his policies and actions, and he had no patience for disloyal Americans. Yet he recognized that McCarthy was a *demagogue*, stirring up anti-Communist hysteria and making false charges to gain power and notoriety. He quietly opposed McCarthy's excesses, but had no power to end his congressional investigations. McCarthy's

Senator Joseph McCarthy holds papers that he claims identify 57 Communist party members in the Truman administration's State Department. After Truman left the presidency, the Senate censured McCarthy for his false and reckless accusations.

downfall came only after Truman left office. During televised investigations of supposed Communists in the army, McCarthy's ugly tactics were finally exposed. In 1954 the Senate *censured* (officially condemned) McCarthy, and his power was broken.

An Assassination Attempt ————————————

In early 1948, the leg of a grand piano sank through the flooring in the White House living quarters. Inspectors who came to investigate the incident soon determined that the old mansion was no longer safe. The White House had been redecorated may times, but no serious work had been done on its underlying structure for more than a century. Major reconstruction was required, so the Trumans moved to Blair House, a comfortable mansion across the street, where they lived until early 1952.

At about 2 p.m. on November 1, 1950, an usually hot autumn day in Washington, two armed Puerto Rican nationalists, Oscar Collazo and Griselio Torresola, approached Blair House from opposite directions, guns drawn. They hoped to overpower the guards outside, enter the house, and assassinate the president to promote the cause of Puerto Rican independence. At the time, Truman was napping in an upstairs room. The guards were ready, however, and exchanged several shots with the attackers. Within moments, Torresola and one guard lay dead, and Collazo, seriously wounded, was taken into custody.

Despite the attempt on his life, Truman went about his day's activities as if nothing special had happened. "A president has to expect those things," he later remarked. Collazo was sentenced to death, but the president commuted his sentence

On November 1, 1950, two Puerto Rican nationalists stormed Blair House, where the Truman family was living, hoping to kill the president. Guards shot both of them on the sidewalk outside the house (A and B). Truman peeked out the second-floor window (C) after the shooting ended.

to life in prison. In 1979 he was pardoned by President Jimmy Carter and released from prison.

Truman vs. MacArthur ——————————

By March 1951, the fighting in Korea had settled into a stalemate. General Douglas MacArthur, leader of the UN forces, was impatient. He had been horrified when Chinese Communist troops entered the war, and he believed that the United States had the opportunity to stop the Chinese once and for all. If they

---

Television

The first network television shows were broadcast in 1946, and in the following years millions of Americans bought a television set for the first time. Truman bought the first "television machine," as he called it, for the White House. In 1948, the national political conventions were televised for the first time, and in January 1949, Truman's inauguration was shown live. It attracted ten million viewers, the largest television audience up to that time.

The president's greatest moment on TV was probably the televised tour of the White House he gave on May 3, 1952. The executive mansion had been closed for major repairs for more than three years, and the Trumans had lived in the nearby Blair House. Now the president proudly led the television cameras through the refurbished mansion room by room, commenting on points of interest. At one point, he even paused to play a short piece by Mozart on the piano in the East Room. The critics in the next day's newspapers gave Truman rave reviews.

☆ ☆ ☆

President Truman and General Douglas MacArthur during the Korean War. Truman removed MacArthur from command in April 1951 for publicly criticizing his commander in chief. MacArthur remained popular and returned home to a warm welcome, while Truman's popularity dropped.

weren't stopped here, he said, they would one day overrun all of Asia. He urged President Truman to give him authority to bomb Chinese bases in Manchuria, a Chinese region near the North Korean border. Truman refused. He believed that an attack on Chinese soil could lead to a third world war, involving not only China but also the Soviets with their new atomic bombs.

MacArthur refused to accept the decision of his commander in chief. Instead, he publicly criticized Truman and his war policy. The president was enraged at this flagrant act of *insubordination*, MacArthur's refusal to obey an order from his commander in chief. On April 11, 1951, he removed MacArthur from command of the UN forces in Korea.

Many Americans came to MacArthur's defense. Militant anti-Communists promoted him as a special hero with the courage to be really tough on Communism. A few conservative Republicans called for Truman's impeachment. MacArthur returned to a hero's welcome in the United States, where he even addressed a joint session of Congress.

Although Truman's action against MacArthur was unpopular, a Senate committee investigated the matter and issued a report supporting the president. Later events showed that Communist Chinese armies never did overrun Asia as MacArthur feared. More important, MacArthur had broken a firm and fast military rule by refusing to accept a lawful order by his commander in chief.

No Third Term

As the Korean War plodded on with no end in sight, Truman faced the worst months of his administration. By November 1951, his public opinion polls showed that only 23 percent of the public approved of his performance. The president was tired of the barrage of criticism and weary of Washington.

On March 29, 1952, Truman announced that he would not seek another term as president. "I have served my country long and I think efficiently and honestly," he said. "I do not feel that it is my duty to spend another four years in the White House."

The Steel Strike —————————————————

In the last months of his term, Truman faced one further disappointment. In November 1951, the steelworkers' union demanded a pay raise from steel companies. At first, the company owners refused to negotiate. Later, the parties negotiated for three months, but made no progress. The steelworkers announced that they would strike, beginning a minute after midnight on April 9, 1952.

Steel was necessary to manufacture tanks, arms, and ammunition for the war in Korea. In addition, Truman was angry that the steelmakers refused to negotiate in good faith with the workers. To protect national security, he decided to take executive action. At the moment the strike began, the government took over operation of the steel plants. This action brought a barrage of harsh criticism.

The steel industry sued to regain control of its plants, and the case went to the Supreme Court in May. The Court ruled in favor of the steel companies by a 6 to 3 vote and ordered the government to give up control of the plants. The majority found that Truman had exceeded his authority by seizing the steel plants without the approval of Congress. Even if Truman's intentions were good, seizure of private business by the chief executive set a dangerous precedent. It was a humiliating moment for Truman. When the owners took back the plants, the workers

General Dwight D. Eisenhower was commander of Allied forces in Europe during World War II and later was the first commander of the NATO alliance. In 1952 he was nominated for president by the Republican party and was elected in November.

★ BATTLES AT HOME AND ABROAD ★

went out on strike and remained out for seven weeks, the longest steel strike in U.S. history, before a settlement was reached.

The Election of 1952 ——————————————

At the Democratic presidential convention in July 1952, Truman supported the candidacy of Adlai Stevenson, governor of Illinois, who went on to win the nomination. Douglas MacArthur ran briefly for the Republican nomination for president, but he was not a serious contender. The Republicans nominated another World War II general and the first NATO commander, Dwight Eisenhower. After 20 years of Democratic rule, the nation was ready for a change, and voters elected Eisenhower and his vice-presidential candidate, Richard Nixon.

For the Trumans, inauguration day in January 1953 began on a sour note. The Eisenhowers refused to have lunch with the Trumans and even refused to have coffee with them in the White House before the inaugural ceremonies. As Eisenhower and his wife Mamie waited in the car to go to the inauguration, Truman fumed over this slight and only swallowed his anger after Bess insisted. Soon after the ceremonies, the Trumans boarded the train that would carry them home to Independence and a welcome retirement.

Chapter 6

Author Truman —————————————

Harry and Bess Truman were happy to return to the only home that they had known all their married life—the stately Victorian house at 219 North Delaware in Independence.

Now a private citizen, Truman worked nearly as hard in retirement as he had as president. He published two volumes of memoirs in quick succession, *Years of Decision* (1955) and *Years of Trial and Hope* (1956). *Life* magazine paid him $600,000 for the exclusive rights to publish excerpts. The income from the magazine and book publications gave the former president financial security for his old age. In 1960 he wrote a third book, *Mr. Citizen*, an autobiography. Only two earlier presidents, Calvin Coolidge and Herbert Hoover, had written and published about their presidencies during their lifetimes.

Harry and Bess Truman retired to this spacious house in Independence, Missouri. It had been owned by Bess's grandparents and by her mother. The Trumans considered it their home from 1919 to their deaths, even when they were spending most of each year in Washington, D.C.

A Presidential Library

The project dearest to Truman's heart was his presidential library. The city of

Independence donated a 13-acre (5-ha) park for the site, and Truman's friends

contributed to its building costs. The Harry S. Truman Library was dedicated in

July 1957. It houses Truman's presidential papers and memorabilia from his years in the White House. Truman also spoke up for preserving the papers of earlier presidents. Through his efforts, Congress agreed to index all existing presidential papers and preserve them on microfilm.

Truman's daily routine back in Independence was unchanged from his early days living there. He rose at 5:30 and took his morning walk of one and a half miles (2.4 km). He greeted neighbors along his route, stopped for a few words with passersby, and even paused long enough to sign autographs for admirers. He returned home for breakfast and was at his office desk in the Truman Library by 8:45 sharp. He often arrived before the regular staff and answered the phones. Callers would be startled to be greeted by the former president saying, "This is the old man himself."

A Presidential Best Seller

In the summer of 1961, Truman was interviewed at length by writer Merle Miller for a series of television films about his presidency. Two years after Truman's death, in 1974, Miller published the interviews, along with material from Truman's friends and associates. The book was called *Plain Speaking: An Oral Biography of Harry S. Truman*, and it captured Truman's warmth, wit, and down-to-earth character far better than the three books he wrote himself. *Plain Speaking* became an instant best seller. Truman became more popular than he had been during his presidency.

☆★☆

Family ——————————————————————

Among the highlights of Harry and Bess Truman's retirement years were the marriage of their daughter Margaret and the birth of four grandsons. After Truman left the White House, Margaret moved to New York, where she worked in broadcasting. In 1956 she married Clifton Daniel, a writer and later an editor for the *New York Times*. The Trumans enjoyed visiting the growing Daniel family in New York and in hosting visits from them in Independence.

Margaret Truman Daniel began a biography of her father during his last years, and it was published in 1973, soon after his death. She later became a successful writer of mysteries, beginning with *Murder in the White House* (1980). Nearly all of her later mysteries were set in or near familiar Washington landmarks.

A Final Vindication ——————————————————

During Eisenhower's presidency, the coolness between him and Harry Truman continued. The new president never consulted Truman and never invited him to the White House, even for ceremonial occasions. When Democrat John F. Kennedy became president in 1961, he invited the Trumans to visit the White House for the first time in eight years. Then in 1963, Lyndon Johnson became president. Johnson valued Truman's advice, and in 1965 he paid Truman a particular tribute.

In July 1965, the Medicare Act, providing federal medical coverage for the elderly, was passed by Congress. Johnson arranged to sign the bill into law at the Truman Library in Independence with Harry Truman at his side. Twenty years earlier Truman had proposed a federal health insurance program for the elderly, but had not been able to get it passed. After the ceremony, Truman told Johnson, "You have made me a very, very happy man."

Last Years

By 1970, Truman's health began to fail. He entered the Research Hospital and Medical Center in Kansas City in early December 1972 with a lung infection. He grew increasingly weaker, and died on December 26, 1972, at age 88. Former president Johnson, who attended his funeral, said of him, "Few men of any time ever shaped the world as did the man from Independence." Johnson himself died three weeks later of a heart attack.

Truman was buried in the courtyard of the Truman Library. Ten years later Bess died at the age of 97 and was buried at his side.

Legacy

On his desk in the oval office of the White House, President Truman had two mottoes displayed. One said "Always Do Right," a quote from Missouri-born writer Mark Twain. The other said "The Buck Stops Here." Truman believed fiercely that the chief executive must take responsibility for his decisions and actions, and that he must never "pass the buck," letting someone else take the blame. Truman's sign, and his willingness to live by its message, is one of his enduring legacies.

Among his decisions as president, none was more fateful than the order to drop the first atomic bombs on Japan in 1945. Whether dropping the bomb saved more lives in the end than it took is still debatable. So is the morality of the action. Truman understood the unimagined destructiveness of the bomb and knew that he was introducing a terrible new kind of weapon to the world, but he never showed any doubt that he had made the right decision. During the Cold War, nuclear weapons became a useful *deterrent* to (a strong reason against) war, and in the 60 years after World War II no nation used the weapons in wartime.

A second fateful decision was to send thousands of U.S. troops to South Korea to oppose its invasion by North Korea. Critics point out that after nearly three years of fighting, that war ended without a clear-cut victory. Still, Truman's actions sent a clear message that the West would strongly oppose efforts of Communist nations to take new territory by force.

Harry Truman at the Truman Library, still displaying the famous sign from his White House desk: "The Buck Stops Here!"

Truman's Achievements

Other achievements of Truman's presidency have been almost universally praised. His support of civil rights was courageous, coming at a time when segregation and racism were accepted by many Americans. No other president between Abraham Lincoln and Lyndon Johnson made civil rights such an important priority. Truman took his stand even though it cost him the support of many in his own party and might have cost his election to a full term.

Even though a hostile Congress refused to pass many of his domestic programs, he still did a surprising amount of good. He eased the way to postwar prosperity in America by continuing the G.I. Bill of 1944, helping 8 million veterans to gain further education to prepare for civilian careers and buy homes with loans guaranteed by the government. Truman also increased Social Security benefits for the elderly and disabled.

Still, Truman's most important of contributions were in foreign affairs. Facing a powerful challenge from Communist nations, he announced clearly that Western nations would meet the political, economic, and military threat. The Truman Doctrine promised U.S. aid to nations facing the threat of Communist takeover. The Marshall Plan offered billions of dollars to help European nations rebuild after the calamity of World War II. The formation of NATO helped arm

President Harry Truman.

Europe against any attack by the Soviet Union and its Communist allies. In 1949, Truman stood up against the threat of the Soviets to take over Berlin by ordering the Berlin airlift, and the following year he opposed the Communist invasion of South Korea.

At the same time, Truman kept his sense of perspective. His administration worked closely with the United Nations to address other trouble spots in the world. He rejected General MacArthur's extreme views urging military attacks on Communist China. At home, he also rejected the extreme views of Senator Joseph McCarthy, who used anti-Communism to accuse and humiliate Americans he disagreed with.

When Truman took office, many considered him a mediocre and uneducated man. His actions as president showed that he was a close student of history and took a long view of the future of the United States. He also had a firm sense of morality and never consulted public opinion polls before making big decisions. "It isn't polls or public opinion of the moment that counts," he said. "It's right and wrong."

Truman made his mistakes. Early in his administration, he supported a program promoted by anti-Communists to require government employees to take loyalty oaths. The program was later used to blacken the reputations of innocent people. Later, Truman overstepped his authority as president by ordering a government takeover of the steel companies. Near the end of his administration, it was revealed that friends he had appointed to a government finance agency had used their positions for personal profit.

A Great President

On balance, Truman's performance as president during a difficult and tumultuous time has earned wide praise from historians. "The responsibilities he bore were like those of no other president before him," writes David McCullough in his monumental biography of Truman, "and he more than met the test."

It is Truman's courage, his forthrightness, and his simple honesty that Americans continue to admire. These remain qualities we look for in our leaders. Neglected and unappreciated in office, Truman is ranked today among the greatest of presidents. He himself never saw it that way. "I wasn't one of the great presidents," he said soon after leaving the White House, "but I had a good time trying to be, I can tell you that."

Fast Facts Harry S. Truman

Birth:	May 8, 1884
Birthplace:	Lamar, Missouri
Parents:	John Anderson Truman and Martha Ellen Young Truman
Brothers & Sisters:	Vivian (1886–1965)
	Mary Jane (1889–1978)
Education:	Independence High School, graduated 1901
	Kansas City School of Law, attended 1923–1925
Occupation:	Farmer, merchant, county judge
Marriage:	To Elizabeth Wallace on June 28, 1919
Children:	(see First Lady Fast Facts at right)
Political Party:	Democratic
Public Offices:	1914 Road Overseer of Jackson County
	1915 Postmaster of Grandview
	1923–1924 County Judge, Jackson County
	1927–1933 Presiding Judge, Jackson County
	1935–1945 U.S. Senator from Missouri
	1945 Vice President under President Franklin D. Roosevelt
	1945–1953 33rd President of the United States
His Vice President:	Alben Barkley (1949–1953)
Major Actions as President:	1945 Ordered atom bombs dropped on Japan to end WW II
	1947 Announced Truman Doctrine to protect democracy in Western Europe
	1948 Established Marshall Plan for the economic recovery of war-torn Europe
	1949 Helped set up the North Atlantic Treaty Organization (NATO)
	1950 Ordered American troops into Korea
	1951 Relieved General Douglas MacArthur as UN commander in Korea
	1952 Seized the steel industry to end strike of steelworkers
Firsts:	First president to deliver a televised speech from the White House
	First president to have a television in the White House
	First former president to address Congress
Death:	December 26, 1972, in Kansas City, Missouri
Age at Death:	88 years
Burial Place:	Truman Library, Independence, Missouri

Fast Facts

Elizabeth (Bess) Wallace Truman

Birth:	February 13, 1885
Birthplace:	Independence, Missouri
Parents:	David Willock Wallace and Madge Gates Wallace
Brothers & Sisters:	Three younger brothers: Frank, George, and David (known as Fred)
Education:	Independence High School, graduated 1901
	Miss Barstow's Finishing School for Girls, Kansas City, Missouri
Marriage:	To Harry S. Truman on June 28, 1919
Children:	Mary Margaret Truman (1924–)
Firsts:	Oversaw renovations of the White House for first time since Monroe administration
Died:	October 18, 1982
Age at Death:	97 years
Burial Place:	Truman Library, Independence, Missouri

Timeline

1884	1890	1901	1907	1914
Harry S. Truman born in Lamar, Missouri, May 8.	Truman family moves to Independence, Missouri.	Truman graduates from high school.	Moves to Grandview, Missouri, to help his father run the family farm.	Father dies; World War I begins in Europe.

1926	1930	1932	1934	1940
Elected presiding judge of Jackson County.	Great Depression beings; Truman re-elected presiding judge.	Franklin Delano Roosevelt elected president.	Truman elected to the U.S. Senate from Missouri.	Truman re-elected to the Senate; Roosevelt re-elected to third term.

1948	1949	1950	1951	1952
Congress approves the Marshall Plan, offering aid for reconstruction in Europe; Truman elected to a full term as president.	Helps establish the North Atlantic Treaty Organization (NATO).	Gains UN approval for assistance to South Korea after its invasion by North Korea, June; U.S. forces enter combat.	Truman removes General Douglas MacArthur as commander of UN forces in Korea, April.	Announces he will not run for re-election, March; seizes the steel industry to end a strike, April; Supreme Court orders an end to steel plant seizures, May.

1917	**1918**	**1919**	**1922**	**1924**

U.S. enters World War; Truman enlists.

Serves with distinction in France.

Returns home; marries Bess Wallace, June 28; opens a men's clothing shop in Kansas City.

Clothing shop fails; Truman elected county judge in Jackson County.

Daughter Margaret born, February 17; Truman defeated for re-election, November.

1941	**1944**	**1945**	**1945**	**1947**

U.S. declares war on Japan after Japanese attack on Pearl Harbor, December.

Truman nominated for vice president on ticket with President Roosevelt; elected, November.

Roosevelt dies suddenly, April 12; Truman sworn in as president.

War in Europe ends, May 7; Truman orders use of atomic bombs against Japan; war in Asia ends August 14.

Congress approves the Truman Doctrine, promising aid to countries threatened by Communism.

1953	**1957**	**1965**	**1972**

Republican Dwight Eisenhower inaugurated president; Truman retires to Independence, Missouri.

The Truman Presidential Library is dedicated in July.

President Lyndon Johnson signs new Medicare bill at the Truman Library.

Truman dies, December 26.

Glossary

blockade: restricting the flow of supplies by a government to put pressure on its adversaries; the Soviet Union restricted the flow of supplies into West Berlin in 1948 and 1949

censure: a formal condemnation of a government official by a legislature or other official body

demagogue: a leader who plays on the fears and prejudices of people to gain power and attention

deterrent: something that will discourage or prevent a person or group from an action; atomic weapons are a *deterrent* to the warlike behavior of other nations

haberdashery: a shop selling men's clothing and accessories

inflation: a rise in prices for necessary goods which results in a decline in the value of the currency

insubordination: disobedience to one's superior, especially in a military organization

platform: in politics, a written document stating the principles and aims of a party, on which candidates can "stand" when campaigning for office

Prohibition: in U.S. history, the period between 1919 and 1933, when the manufacture, sale, or use of alcoholic beverages was prohibited by law

stroke: a blockage of blood flow in the brain, which may cause paralysis or death

Further Reading

Anthony, Carl Sferrazza. *America's First Families: An Inside View of 200 Years of Private Life in the White House.* New York: Touchstone, 2000.

Blassingame, Wyatt. *The Look-It-Up Book of Presidents.* New York: Random House, 1996.

Morris, Jeffrey Brandon. *The Truman Way.* Minneapolis: Lerner Publications, 1995.

Paletta, Lu Ann, and Fred L. Worth. *The World Almanac of Presidential Facts.* New York: World Almanac, 1988.

Schuman, Michael A. *Harry S. Truman.* Berkeley Heights, NJ: Enslow Publishers, 2003.

Truman, Harry S. *The Wit and Wisdom of Harry S. Truman.* Edited by Ralph Keyes. New York: Gramercy Books, 1999.

Whitney, David C., and Robin Vaughn Whitney. *The American Presidents.* 8th edition. Pleasantville, NY: Reader's Digest Association, 1996.

MORE ADVANCED READING

McCullough, David G. *Truman.* New York: Simon & Schuster, 1992.

Miller, Merle. *Plain Speaking: An Oral Biography of Harry S. Truman.* New York: Berkley, 1974.

Truman, Harry S. *The Autobiography of Harry S. Truman.* Columbia, MO: University of Missouri Press, 2002.

Truman, Margaret. *Harry S. Truman.* New York: Morrow, 1973.

Places to Visit

★ ★ ★ ★ ★

**Harry S. Truman Birthplace State
Historic Site**
1009 Truman Street
Lamar, MO 64759
(417) 682-2279

The birthplace of Truman, where he lived the first year of his life.

Harry S. Truman Farm Home
12301 Blue Ridge Boulevard
Grandview, MO 64030
(816) 254-7199

The home of Truman's grandparents, where he lived and worked on the farm from 1906 to 1917.

Harry S. Truman National Historic Site
Delaware Street off Truman Road
Independence, MO 64050
(816) 254-9929

The home the Trumans lived in from their marriage to their deaths, except for their years in Washington.

Truman Presidential Museum and Library
500 West US Highway 24
Independence, MO 64050
(800) 833-1225

This site features exhibits about Truman's life and presidency, audiovisual presentations, and a replica of Truman's oval office in the White House. The library contains his presidential papers. Harry and Bess Truman are buried in the courtyard.

The White House
1600 Pennsylvania Avenue NW
Washington, DC 20500
Visitors' Office: (202) 456-7041

Truman lived and worked here as 33rd president from 1945 to 1953.

Online Sites of Interest

⭐ **The American Presidency**

http://ap.grolier.com/browse?type=profiles#pres

Concise biographies of Truman from several online encyclopedias, including the Grolier Multimedia Encyclopedia and Encyclopedia Americana.

⭐ **Presidential Inaugural Addresses**

http://www.bartleby.com/124/pres53.html

Truman's complete inaugural address is here as well as access to the inaugural address of every other president.

⭐ **Truman Presidential Museum & Library**

http://www.trumanlibrary.org

Contains a detailed biography of the 33rd president, biographical sketches of Bess and Margaret Truman, a Kids Page, and information about the Truman Museum and Library and its many exhibits.

⭐ **The White House**

http://www.whitehouse.gov/history/presidents/ht33.html

A biography of Harry Truman. The site also contains information about the current president and vice president, White House history and tours, a virtual tour of the historic building, current events, trivia quizzes, and much more.

Table of Presidents

	1. George Washington	2. John Adams	3. Thomas Jefferson	4. James Madison
Took office	Apr 30 1789	Mar 4 1797	Mar 4 1801	Mar 4 1809
Left office	Mar 3 1797	Mar 3 1801	Mar 3 1809	Mar 3 1817
Birthplace	Westmoreland Co, VA	Braintree, MA	Shadwell, VA	Port Conway, VA
Birth date	Feb 22 1732	Oct 20 1735	Apr 13 1743	Mar 16 1751
Death date	Dec 14 1799	July 4 1826	July 4 1826	June 28 1836

	9. William H. Harrison	10. John Tyler	11. James K. Polk	12. Zachary Taylor
Took office	Mar 4 1841	Apr 6 1841	Mar 4 1845	Mar 5 1849
Left office	**Apr 4 1841•**	Mar 3 1845	Mar 3 1849	**July 9 1850•**
Birthplace	Berkeley, VA	Greenway, VA	Mecklenburg Co, NC	Barboursville, VA
Birth date	Feb 9 1773	Mar 29 1790	Nov 2 1795	Nov 24 1784
Death date	Apr 4 1841	Jan 18 1862	June 15 1849	July 9 1850

	17. Andrew Johnson	18. Ulysses S. Grant	19. Rutherford B. Hayes	20. James A. Garfield
Took office	Apr 15 1865	Mar 4 1869	Mar 5 1877	Mar 4 1881
Left office	Mar 3 1869	Mar 3 1877	Mar 3 1881	**Sept 19 1881•**
Birthplace	Raleigh, NC	Point Pleasant, OH	Delaware, OH	Orange, OH
Birth date	Dec 29 1808	Apr 27 1822	Oct 4 1822	Nov 19 1831
Death date	July 31 1875	July 23 1885	Jan 17 1893	Sept 19 1881

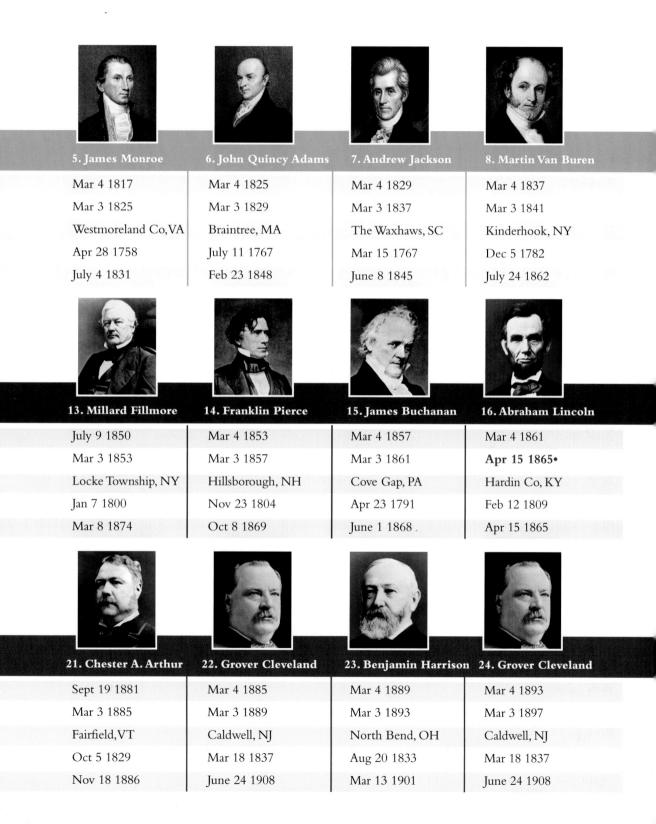

5. James Monroe

Mar 4 1817

Mar 3 1825

Westmoreland Co, VA

Apr 28 1758

July 4 1831

6. John Quincy Adams

Mar 4 1825

Mar 3 1829

Braintree, MA

July 11 1767

Feb 23 1848

7. Andrew Jackson

Mar 4 1829

Mar 3 1837

The Waxhaws, SC

Mar 15 1767

June 8 1845

8. Martin Van Buren

Mar 4 1837

Mar 3 1841

Kinderhook, NY

Dec 5 1782

July 24 1862

13. Millard Fillmore

July 9 1850

Mar 3 1853

Locke Township, NY

Jan 7 1800

Mar 8 1874

14. Franklin Pierce

Mar 4 1853

Mar 3 1857

Hillsborough, NH

Nov 23 1804

Oct 8 1869

15. James Buchanan

Mar 4 1857

Mar 3 1861

Cove Gap, PA

Apr 23 1791

June 1 1868

16. Abraham Lincoln

Mar 4 1861

Apr 15 1865•

Hardin Co, KY

Feb 12 1809

Apr 15 1865

21. Chester A. Arthur

Sept 19 1881

Mar 3 1885

Fairfield, VT

Oct 5 1829

Nov 18 1886

22. Grover Cleveland

Mar 4 1885

Mar 3 1889

Caldwell, NJ

Mar 18 1837

June 24 1908

23. Benjamin Harrison

Mar 4 1889

Mar 3 1893

North Bend, OH

Aug 20 1833

Mar 13 1901

24. Grover Cleveland

Mar 4 1893

Mar 3 1897

Caldwell, NJ

Mar 18 1837

June 24 1908

25. William McKinley

Took office	Mar 4 1897
Left office	**Sept 14 1901•**
Birthplace	Niles, OH
Birth date	Jan 29 1843
Death date	Sept 14 1901

26. Theodore Roosevelt

Took office	Sept 14 1901
Left office	Mar 3 1909
Birthplace	New York, NY
Birth date	Oct 27 1858
Death date	Jan 6 1919

27. William H. Taft

Took office	Mar 4 1909
Left office	Mar 3 1913
Birthplace	Cincinnati, OH
Birth date	Sept 15 1857
Death date	Mar 8 1930

28. Woodrow Wilson

Took office	Mar 4 1913
Left office	Mar 3 1921
Birthplace	Staunton, VA
Birth date	Dec 28 1856
Death date	Feb 3 1924

33. Harry S. Truman

Took office	Apr 12 1945
Left office	Jan 20 1953
Birthplace	Lamar, MO
Birth date	May 8 1884
Death date	Dec 26 1972

34. Dwight D. Eisenhower

Took office	Jan 20 1953
Left office	Jan 20 1961
Birthplace	Denison, TX
Birth date	Oct 14 1890
Death date	Mar 28 1969

35. John F. Kennedy

Took office	Jan 20 1961
Left office	**Nov 22 1963•**
Birthplace	Brookline, MA
Birth date	May 29 1917
Death date	Nov 22 1963

36. Lyndon B. Johnson

Took office	Nov 22 1963
Left office	Jan 20 1969
Birthplace	Johnson City, TX
Birth date	Aug 27 1908
Death date	Jan 22 1973

41. George Bush

Took office	Jan 20 1989
Left office	Jan 20 1993
Birthplace	Milton, MA
Birth date	June 12 1924
Death date	—

42. Bill Clinton

Took office	Jan 20 1993
Left office	Jan 20 2001
Birthplace	Hope, AR
Birth date	Aug 19 1946
Death date	—

43. George W. Bush

Took office	Jan 20 2001
Left office	—
Birthplace	New Haven, CT
Birth date	July 6 1946
Death date	—

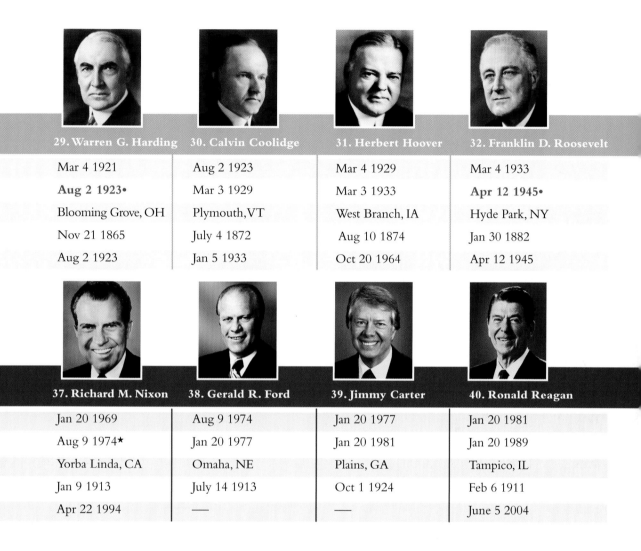

29. Warren G. Harding	30. Calvin Coolidge	31. Herbert Hoover	32. Franklin D. Roosevelt
Mar 4 1921	Aug 2 1923	Mar 4 1929	Mar 4 1933
Aug 2 1923•	Mar 3 1929	Mar 3 1933	**Apr 12 1945•**
Blooming Grove, OH	Plymouth, VT	West Branch, IA	Hyde Park, NY
Nov 21 1865	July 4 1872	Aug 10 1874	Jan 30 1882
Aug 2 1923	Jan 5 1933	Oct 20 1964	Apr 12 1945

37. Richard M. Nixon	38. Gerald R. Ford	39. Jimmy Carter	40. Ronald Reagan
Jan 20 1969	Aug 9 1974	Jan 20 1977	Jan 20 1981
Aug 9 1974★	Jan 20 1977	Jan 20 1981	Jan 20 1989
Yorba Linda, CA	Omaha, NE	Plains, GA	Tampico, IL
Jan 9 1913	July 14 1913	Oct 1 1924	Feb 6 1911
Apr 22 1994	—	—	June 5 2004

• Indicates the president died while in office.

★ Richard Nixon resigned before his term expired.

Index

About the Author

Steven Otfinoski attended Boston University and graduated with a B.A. from Antioch College in Yellow Springs, Ohio. He has written more than a hundred books for young adults and children. He is the author of *William Henry Harrison*, *Abraham Lincoln*, and *Rutherford B. Hayes* in the Encyclopedia of Presidents. Among his most recent books are *African Americans in the Visual Arts*; *African Americans in the Performing Arts*; *Bugsy Siegel and the Postwar Boom*; *John Wilkes Booth and the Civil War*; *Marco Polo: To China and Back*; *Francisco Coronado: In Search of the Seven Cities of Gold*; *Nations in Transition: Afghanistan*; *Nations in Transition: The Baltic Republics*; *It's My State: Washington*; and *Celebrate the States: Georgia*. He has also written two books on popular music for adults—*The Golden Age of Rock Instrumentals* and *The Golden Age of Novelty Songs*.

Mr. Otfinoski lives in Connecticut with his wife Beverly, a teacher and editor, and their two children Daniel and Martha. Among his hobbies are reading, traveling, listening to and collecting popular music of the 1950s and 1960s, and playing tennis.